OPPOSITES
All Around Me!

BIG
and Small

A Crabtree Roots Book

CRABTREE
Publishing Company
www.crabtreebooks.com

School-to-Home Support for Caregivers and Teachers

This book helps children grow by letting them practice reading. Here are a few guiding questions to help the reader with building his or her comprehension skills. Possible answers appear here in red.

Before Reading:

• What do I think this book is about?
  - *This book is about big things and small things.*
  - *This book is about opposites.*

• What do I want to learn about this topic?
  - *I want to learn what big things look like.*
  - *I want to learn what is big and what is small.*

During Reading:

• I wonder why...
  - *I wonder why some trees grow really big.*
  - *I wonder why mice are small.*

• What have I learned so far?
  - *I have learned that elephants are big.*
  - *I have learned what a small boat and a big boat looks like.*

After Reading:

• What details did I learn about this topic?
  - *I have learned that trees can be many different sizes.*
  - *I have learned that boats can be big or small.*

• Read the book again and look for the vocabulary words.
  - *I see the word **tree** on page 5 and the word **boat** on page 8. The other vocabulary words are found on page 14.*

What is big, and
what is **small**?

This **tree** is big.

This tree is small.

This **boat** is big.

This boat is small.

An **elephant** is big.

A **mouse** is small.

Word List

Sight Words

a	big	what
an	is	
and	this	

Words to Know

boat　**elephant**　**mouse**

small　**tree**

31 Words

What is big, and what is **small**?

This **tree** is big.

This tree is small.

This **boat** is big

This boat is small.

An **elephant** is big.

A **mouse** is small.

Written by: Amy Culliford

Designed by: Rhea Wallace

Series Development: James Earley

Proofreader: Ellen Rodger

Educational Consultant: Marie Lemke M.Ed.

Photographs:
Shutterstock: Erik Lam: cover; Kanusommer: p. 1;
    Sam Wordley: p. 3, 14; Sergey Berestetsky: p. 4, 14;
    Smit: p. 7; Resul Muslu: p. 8, 14; Pierre-Olivier: p. 9;
    Fotogrin: p. 10, 14; Rudmer Zwerver: p. 12, 14

Library and Archives Canada Cataloguing in Publication

Title: Big and small / Amy Culliford.
Names: Culliford, Amy, 1992- author.
Description: Series statement: Opposites all around me! | "A
Crabtree roots book".
  Identifiers: Canadiana (print) 20210159464 | Canadiana (ebook)
20210159472 | ISBN 9781427140166
(hardcover) | ISBN 9781427140227 (softcover) | ISBN 9781427133540
(HTML) | ISBN 9781427140289
(read-along ebook) | ISBN 9781427134141 (EPUB)
Subjects: LCSH: Size judgment—Juvenile literature. | LCSH: Size perception—
Juvenile literature.
LCSH: Polarity—Juvenile literature. | LCSH: English language—Synonyms
and antonyms—Juvenile literature.
Classification: LCC BF299.S5 C85 2021 | DDC j153.7/52—dc23

Library of Congress Cataloging-in-Publication Data

Names: Culliford, Amy, 1992- author.
Title: Big and small / Amy Culliford.
  Description: New York, NY : Crabtree Publishing Company, [2022] |
  Series: Opposites all around me! a Crabtree roots book | Includes index.
  | Audience: Ages 4-6 | Audience: Grades K-1
Identifiers: LCCN 2021010792 (print) | LCCN 2021010793 (ebook) |
  ISBN 9781427140166 (hardcover) | ISBN 9781427140227 (paperback) |
  ISBN 9781427133540 (ebook) | ISBN 9781427134141 (epub) | I
  ISBN 9781427140289
  (read along)
Subjects: LCSH: Size perception--Juvenile literature. | Size
  judgment--Juvenile literature. | Polarity--Juvenile literature. |
  English language--Synonyms and antonyms--Juvenile literature.
Classification: LCC BF299.S5 C85 2022 (print) | LCC BF299.S5 (ebook) |
  DDC 153.7/52--dc23
LC record available at https://lccn.loc.gov/2021010792
LC ebook record available at https://lccn.loc.gov/2021010793

Crabtree Publishing Company

www.crabtreebooks.com   1-800-387-7650   Printed in the U.S.A./062021/CG20210401

Published in the United States
Crabtree Publishing
347 Fifth Avenue, Suite 1402-145
New York, NY, 10016

Published in Canada
Crabtree Publishing
616 Welland Ave.
St. Catharines, Ontario L2M 5V6